For our memories – memories held dearly and memories lost, memories of loved ones and the memories of us in the hearts of those we love.

    Natalie Kormos

Susan Ross Parish and I were a couple for over fifty years. We enjoyed wandering through many art galleries around the world. Only during the last few years of her Alzheimer's journey did she show any interest in making her own art. Through the advice of a friend we were introduced to the wonderful art therapist Annalisa. Once a week for a couple of years, under the caring guidance of Annalisa, they produced at least a couple of hundred amazing pieces. During the rest of the week Susan would sit at her desk for hours a day working on her own. The making of art gave her considerable joy and purpose. Over that time, I photographed, named and digitized well over 600 of what I considered to be significant pieces. Susan had a pure heart and inspired all who knew her. She would have been so honoured to know that her efforts have been incorporated amongst Natalie's beautiful words in "Fibres of a Memory".

    Brian Parish

A memory is a ray of sunshine, streaming through the trees,
The excitement of an adventure, a whispering ocean breeze.

A star that never fades, twinkling in our heart,
Between our loved ones, from which our minds can never depart.

A light that outshines the sun, and glistens through the darkest night,
As carefree as the dancing tail, on a sailing kite.

Crisp autumn leaves, dancing in the wind,
Begin falling in swirling spirals, as the world continues to spin.

The golden dusk of a summer evening, before the sun is set to sleep,
A soft blanket of snow gently falling,
beneath which the world shall keep.

The pattering of fragrant rain, spilling from the clouds,
Colourful umbrellas, and raincoats enshroud.

Waves that gently come up, to meet the sun-warmed sand,
She sits beside me, the two of us hand in hand.

The breath off the ocean, blowing lightly through her hair,
Dancing in the falling leaves, are memories we do share.

She walks beside me under the umbrella, her hand in mine,
Smiling up at me with not a care, stopping the turning hands of time.

In her eyes I find the warmth of spring, resounding with a laughing glint,
Her smile the soft kiss of summer, a timeless loveliness does hint.

Smiling as if knowing the hands of time, could never grasp our love,
As if we danced to a clock all of our own, each other's hearts beloved.

Though it is perhaps those so young at heart,
on which cruel tricks time does play,
Stealing away fragments so dear, our noble minds begin to fray.

Though our hearts may be strong, beating for a battle to be won,
Things we may encounter, from which we are unable to run.

No fault of our own, nor of those that stand by our side,
It comes not as a raging storm, from which we can hide.

Not bursting into our lives, as a rampage of swirling soot,
Nor flames licking at our sides, to be stamped out by foot.

The cruelest way, by which to be robbed of thought,
Instead comes as a mist, a photograph with a blurred spot.

A fog through which, there lies no guiding light,
A grounded bird, never again to take flight.

A puzzle that keeps losing pieces, each time it's made to be whole,
The sun-blushed summer slowly blotted out,
by the winter's coming cold.

My memories used to flow, as free as the wild spring breeze,
Recalling a smile from a day long ago, used to come with such ease.

Now each morning, as my eyes open to the coming day,
The ticking hands of the teasing clock, its laughs in my mind do play.

No sense of excitement, nor fleeting bursts of joy,
No eagerness to meet the day, no agenda I employ.

But this mustn't have always been this way, not always so very bland,
Were there not golden times I remember, days so very grand?

But though I sit quietly, with my mind working up a storm,
My thoughts swirl as shadows, never taking solid form.

So as each day slips past me, leaving me exhausted inside,
With my thoughts travelling no further, to myself I bide.

As darkness covers over, and I surrender to my sleep,
Shimmery fragments of light, into my mind do creep.

So very many birthday parties, and wishes on candles made,
Memories of long ago, I very wish had stayed.

Tears from bullies, and scratches on my knee,
Of chocolate cake and ice cream, and sipping piping tea.

The very moments, of first flying in a plane,
Of lakes and rivers, so many I knew by name.

I could picture the vivid memories, of family travel around the world,
In these moments of peaceful sleep, my life became unfurled.

And it is in these hours, as the world lies asleep,
That parts of me are welcomed back, in my livened dreams they keep.

But then with the rising of the sun, the shimmers are blotted out,
No gleaming times play in my head, no youthful adventures spout.

In these days there are faces, many that come and go,
Yet though I strain my eyes, none recognised that I know.

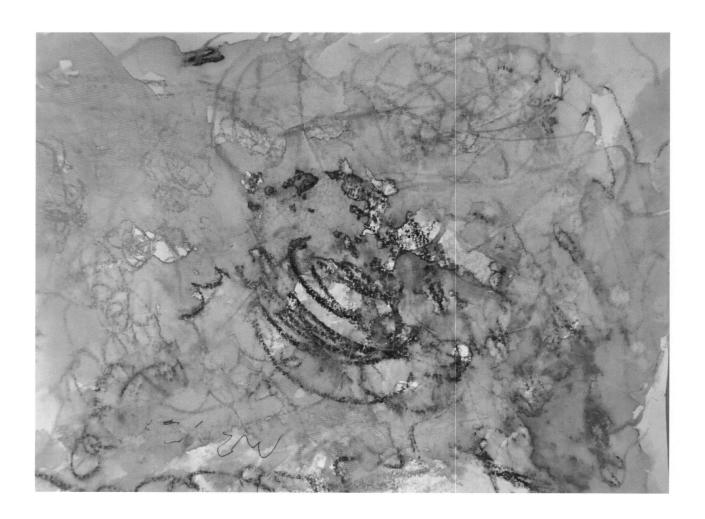

I sit in my rocking chair, outside in the light breeze,
Murmurs of thoughts, none of which I can seize.

I see what lies before me, though I know not what had the day before,
As if peeping beneath the slivered crack, of a shut and fastened door.

Try though I may, to think why I am where I sit,
Is a jagged puzzle piece, into the picture it does not fit.

My mind seems as if, a whisper lost in a howling wind,
Blotted out by the hammering rain, on a roof of tin.

I try to relax my mind, and settle my swirling thoughts,
In hopes that when still, some memories can be caught.

I allow the storm inside my head, to slip silently away,
A weathered ship lost at sea, sailing upon a sheltered bay.

And some shadows in my mind, slowly begin to clear,
My hands almost grasping, something so very near.

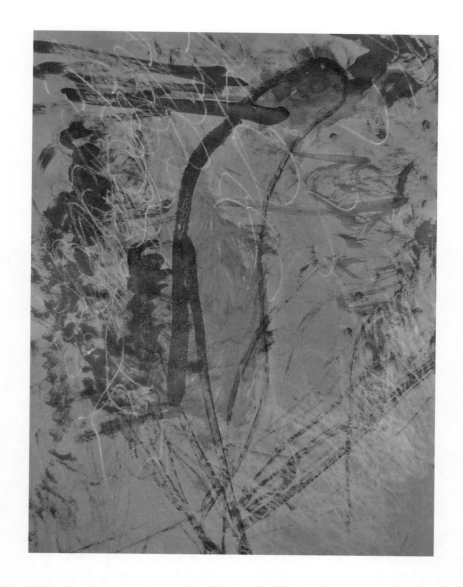

Those green eyes before me, I must have known them once,
Were they only my imagination, living in dreams too many months?

Though they seemed to look at me,
with the certainness beyond a dream,

It was then that I realised,
it was part of a smile from which they gleamed.

And as my focus shifted, beyond the twinkling eyes of green,
Sparkling back into my mind,
was all that for many years, had gone unseen.

A smiling face emerged, patiently looking at me,
Remembering now our time together, adventures so very free.

Something stirred inside of me, that startled my weary heart,
It was as if the very beating, had once again begun to start.

This feeling spread through me, as if warming my sleeping nerves,
Reaching deep inside of me, to all that had been preserved.

Each and every memory, coming to my mind,
Had this lovely face as part of it, always intertwined.

Though my mind was now waking, it suddenly seemed to blur,
Confusion shot through me, as to how this suddenness could occur.

But it was not to my worry, to which answers I did seek,
For it was a quiet tear, that slid silently down my cheek.

As I bowed my head to let it fall, I noticed her hand in mine,
Upon her finger something shimmered, only on the left you could find.

I then remembered all our days, of smiles and sad tears too,

All the warm embraces we shared together,

with so very many I love you's.

Artwork: Susan Parish

Susan Parish didn't let a diagnosis of dementia stop her from living a full life. She took up art in her later years and with the guidance of her art therapist, Annalisa Danowski [(DTATI,RP (CRPO)], created many beautiful works that live on as her legacy. Canadian Susan Parish was a true trailblazer who, by sharing her experiences, pursued her mission to make more communities Dementia Friendly for those living with Alzheimer's. Susan rose to the occasion and let her voice ring out as a guiding beacon of light, 'The whole country should be understanding what Alzheimer's is and what it means to deal with it and live with it. Which is what we're doing, we're living with Alzheimer's'. Creating these pieces of artwork, along with many other paintings, brought Susan great joy and happiness, emotions that are felt by those that continue to view her art. Her beautiful artwork is forever cherished by her family and friends and lives on by being shared with others.

Acknowledgments:

Thank you to Lorraine McCallum for answering my first email, and all those emails to follow, and for connecting me with Brian Parish. Thank you, Brian, for sending the many files of Susan's beautiful artwork, for your faith and excitement in our project and for sharing your kindred memories and stories of Susan. I am deeply honoured to share my poetry alongside the incredible creations of such a wonderful soul. Thank you, Lorraine and Brian, for your patience throughout, as I selected the artworks to accompany my writing, and as I navigated the journey to share this project with others. Thank you to Susan Parish, for the artwork of her beautiful soul and Brian for sharing her story. Thank you to Hayley Boothe, for your encouragement and publishing advice, and to Kemur for creating a network of brilliant horse-loving girls.

Printed in Great Britain
by Amazon

44083419R00023